SUPER SPORTS STAR
MIKE PIAZZA

Michael J. Pellowski

Enslow Publishers, Inc.

40 Industrial Road   PO Box 38
Box 398   Aldershot
Berkeley Heights, NJ 07922 Hants GU12 6BP
USA   UK

http://www.enslow.com

To: Mets Fan, Matt Pellowski

Library of Congress Cataloging-in-Publication Data

Pellowski, Michael.
    Super sports star Mike Piazza / Michael J. Pellowski.
       p. cm. — (Super sports star)
    Summary: Looks at the personal life and professional career of Major League Baseball star Mike Piazza of the New York Mets, who is one of the best hitting catchers in the history of baseball.
    Includes bibliographical references and index.
    ISBN 0-7660-2159-9
    1. Piazza, Mike, 1968–   —Juvenile literature. 2. Baseball players—United States—Biography—Juvenile literature. [1. Piazza, Mike, 1968–   2. Baseball players.] I. Title. II. Series.
    GV865.P52 P45   2004
    796.357'092—dc21

2002155210

Printed in the United States of America

10 9 8 7 6 5 4 3 2 1

Photo Credits: © Jeff Carlick/MLB Photos, p. 24; © 2002 Grieshop/MLB Photos, p. 37; © 1996 Allen Kee/MLB Photos, p. 21; © 1997 Allen Kee/MLB Photos, p. 27; © 2001 Kee/MLB Photos, pp. 4, 7; © 2002 Allen Kee/MLB Photos, p. 35; © MLB Photos, p. 14; © 1998 MLB Photos, p. 28; © 1998 Rich Pilling/MLB Photos, pp. 12, 31, 41; © 2000 Rich Pilling/MLB Photos, p. 18; © 2001 Rich Pilling/MLB Photos, p. 45; © 2002 Rich Pilling/MLB Photos, pp. 1, 9, 33.

Cover Photo: © 2002 Rich Pilling/MLB Photos.

CONTENTS

Introduction

Mike Piazza is a catcher for the New York Mets in the National League of Major League Baseball. He wears No. 31.

When the New York Mets need a key hit, the man they want in the batter's box is Mike Piazza. He is always dangerous at the plate. He is a tough man to get out. Piazza is one of the best-hitting catchers in the history of major league baseball.

The six-foot-three-inch, 215-pound slugger can blast balls deep into the bleachers for home runs. He can hit line drives into gaps in the outfield for extra-base hits. He can hit from foul line to foul line with hard-hit singles. Wherever he hits the ball, Piazza always hustles around the bases.

Piazza only knows one way to play the game he fell in love with as a boy. He gives every play his best effort. He works hard when he is standing beside home plate to bat or crouching behind the plate to catch a pitch.

Piazza is feared by opposing pitchers, respected by his teammates, and loved by millions of fans. New York Mets catcher Mike Piazza is one of major-league baseball's true superstars.

Getting
Hit

On July 8, 2000, Mike Piazza got hit. The Mets were playing an inter-league game against the New York Yankees. On the mound for the Yankees was Roger Clemens. Clemens pitched high and inside to Piazza. The ball hit Piazza in the batting helmet. Piazza's head hurt, and he had to leave the game. The result was bitter feelings between the two New York area teams.

Some Mets players believed Clemens hit Piazza on purpose to get back at him for hitting a grand slam during their June game. Others thought it was an accident. This would not be the end of the controversy between Piazza and Clemens.

Getting hit in the head by a pitch did not slow down Piazza. On July 18, 2000, he tied a Mets record by crushing his third grand slam of the season. The record was first set in 1978 by John Milner. The round-tripper (another name for a home run) came in a game against the Toronto Blue Jays. Piazza then hit his 30th

The 2000 season marked the sixth time Mike Piazza had hit 30 or more home runs in a season.

home run of the season on August 2 in a game against the Houston Astros. The hit marked the sixth straight year Piazza hit 30 or more home runs in a season.

The New York Mets finished the year by placing second in their division. The Atlanta Braves were first. The Mets' record earned them a wild-card spot in the playoffs.

Piazza had a great year. He batted .324 and hit 38 home runs. Piazza also drove in 113 runs.

In the division series against the San Francisco Giants, Piazza had only 3 hits in 14 at bats, for a .214 batting average. But, the Mets beat the Giants, 3–1, to move on to the championship series.

The New York Mets then played for the championship of the National League. In the NL Championship, Piazza batted a sizzling .412 against the Cardinals, collecting 7 hits in 17 at bats. Two of those hits were home runs. He also banged out 3 doubles and drove in 4 runs. The Mets won the championship in five games.

It was on to the 2000 World Series for the New York Mets and Piazza. They were playing a team the Mets knew very well. In fact, the 2000 World Series was an exciting event in baseball history. Two teams from the same city were matched up against each other. The New York Mets faced the American League champion New York Yankees.

Born to Play Baseball

Michael Joseph Piazza was born in Norristown, Pennsylvania, on September 4, 1968. He and his brothers, Vince, Danny, Tony, and Tommy, grew up playing baseball near their home in Phoenixville, Pennsylvania. His father, Vince Piazza, Sr., and his mother, Veronica, wanted their sons to play sports. Their father even helped his boys build a backyard batting cage. Mike spent most of his free time in the batting cage practicing his swing.

Vince Piazza, Sr. was a big baseball fan. One of Vince's childhood friends had grown up to be the manager of a major-league baseball team. That man was Tommy Lasorda, the manager of the Los Angeles Dodgers. Tommy Lasorda was the godfather of Mike's youngest brother, Tommy.

Mike worked as a batboy for the Dodgers whenever Los Angeles traveled to Philadelphia to play the Phillies. Mike met many Dodger stars like Dusty Baker and Steve Garvey.

Mike Piazza and a Mets teammate congratulate each other after a great hit.

Sometimes the pros watched Mike swing a bat and gave him batting tips.

Mike used the tips to make his game better. He played first base and pitched as a kid in Pennsylvania. He was not a catcher. He had tried, but he did not like catching.

When Mike was about twelve years old, his father arranged for him to have a very special visitor. That visitor was Baseball Hall of Famer Ted Williams. Ted Williams had played for the Boston Red Sox. He was one of the greatest hitters in history. In 1941, Williams batted .406 and hit 37 home runs. He was the last major-leaguer to have a .400 batting average.

Ted Williams watched Mike hit. He was very impressed with Mike's hitting skills. Williams predicted Mike would be a great hitter.

At Phoenixville High School, the baseball coach wanted Mike to try out for catcher. A catcher is a team leader. It is a position that takes a lot of athletic skill to play. Good catchers are hard to find. Catchers that can hit well are

★ ★ **UP CLOSE**
★

Baseball Hall of Famer Ted Williams of the Boston Red Sox gave Mike Piazza some batting tips when he was young. Williams was twice voted the Most Valuable Player of the American League. Ted Williams was nicknamed "The Splendid Splinter" because he was tall and thin and had unbelievable athletic ability. Williams died on July 5, 2002, at the age of 83.

even harder to find. But Mike liked playing first base. He did not want to catch. So he did not play varsity baseball until his junior year of high school.

In his second game as a varsity player, Mike cracked a home run that went four hundred feet. He finished his junior year with 12 home runs, which set a school record.

In his last year in high school, Mike clubbed a home run in his first at bat of the season. He finished his senior year batting over .500 and was voted the Most Valuable Player (MVP) of his high school league.

Vince and Veronica wanted their son to go to college. Mike had hopes of playing in the major leagues. Mike hoped he would be selected by a pro team in the amateur player draft.

A draft is when professional teams take turns picking the best players out of high school and college.

Mike wanted a chance to become a major-league star. It was no secret that he hoped to someday play for his favorite team, the Los Angeles Dodgers. But the Dodgers did not draft him. No major-league team wanted the young, hard-hitting first baseman from Pennsylvania. Scouts said Mike was a slow runner. He was not a good defensive player. His throwing arm was too weak.

Mike was disappointed, but he refused to give up his dream of making it to the major leagues. He worked even harder to make his skills better.

CHAPTER 3

A Catcher

Tommy Lasorda helped Mike Piazza find a place to play baseball after high school. Piazza went to the University of Miami in Florida. He became a member of the Hurricanes baseball team.

Piazza did not get a chance to play much baseball for the Miami Hurricanes. He only collected one hit in 9 at bats as a freshman in college. Piazza left the university and transferred to Miami-Dade North Community College. He wanted to play baseball. Piazza's ability and hard work quickly impressed the coaches. Piazza posted a strong .364 batting average in his first year at Miami-Dade North.

Lasorda knew Piazza had the ability to play in the major leagues someday. He spoke with Ben Wade, the director of scouting for the Dodgers. Lasorda begged him to draft the young first baseman. Finally, Wade agreed.

Piazza was drafted in the 62nd round by the Los Angeles Dodgers. He was the 1,389th player selected. In 1988, a total of 1,433 players were drafted.

After Piazza was drafted, he had a tryout at Dodger Stadium. During the tryout, Piazza hit baseballs over the fence into the seats. He starred as a hitter but did not impress Wade as a defensive first baseman.

Lasorda convinced Wade that Mike Piazza could be a catcher. Wade was willing to take a chance on a hard-hitting catcher. So Piazza was signed to play catcher for the Los Angeles Dodgers.

Some baseball experts thought the signing of Piazza was a big joke. People mistakenly thought Piazza was Lasorda's godson and was getting special treatment for that reason.

Ex-major-league catcher Johnny Roseboro, taught Piazza the basics of catching. Piazza worked very hard at his new position. Slowly, his skills behind the plate improved. He learned to like his new position.

Piazza was sent to play for a minor-league

Many thought the signing of Mike Piazza to the Los Angeles Dodgers was a big joke. But Piazza showed them he could really play.

team in Salem, Oregon. Rumors quickly spread among players that Piazza was only on the team because he was Lasorda's pet player. Piazza did not let the rumors upset or anger him. He just kept working hard at hitting baseballs and playing catcher.

In 1990, Piazza played for another minor-league team, the Vero Beach Dodgers. The rumors continued. Piazza could no longer ignore them. He felt so bad that he almost left the team. But Piazza was not a quitter. He refused to give up his dream of making it to the major leagues.

In 1991, Piazza played for a team in Bakersfield, California. He used his bat to silence those who believed his pro career was a joke. He hit .277 and had 124 hits, including 29 home runs.

The following year, Piazza moved up to a better minor-league team where he posted a .377 batting average. Before the season ended, Piazza moved on to an AAA league, which is the last stop in the minors before the major leagues. He hit .341 and hit 16 home runs. At the end of the year, he was brought up to the major leagues to finish out the season as a member of the Los Angeles Dodgers.

★★★ **UP CLOSE**

Mike Piazza's first major-league home run came on September 12, 1992, at Dodger Stadium in Los Angeles. It was hit off pitcher Steve Reed of the San Francisco Giants.

Once again, critics questioned the ability of the young catcher. Sports reporters still joked he was with the Dodgers only because he was Lasorda's friend. In 1993, Piazza silenced the gossip and rumors forever.

Rookie of the Year

Mike Piazza became the Dodgers' starting catcher in 1993. Since he had only played in 21 games the year before, he was still considered a first-year player. He went on to have a terrific season. In his first three months as a starter, he posted a .331 batting average, blasted 15 home runs, and drove in 52 runs.

Piazza also excelled as a catcher. At one point early in his rookie season, he threw out seven base runners in a row attempting to steal. This was the player scouts said had a "weak arm." No one questioned why Piazza was a member of the Dodgers any longer.

When the season ended, Piazza had collected 174 hits in 547 at bats for a .318 batting average. He also hit 35 home runs and had 112 runs batted in. His 35 home runs set a major-league record for the most home runs by a rookie catcher. He also set a Dodger record by throwing out 58 base runners attempting to steal. For his outstanding efforts in 1993, Piazza was named the National League's Rookie of the Year. He was the first Rookie of the Year to drive in more than 100 runs in a season.

Piazza's baseball career took off. In 1994, he was selected to the All-Star team for the second straight year. In each of the next three seasons, he hit over .300 and blasted over 30 home runs.

Catcher Mike Piazza turned in an outstanding effort at the 1996 All-Star Game. The game was held at Veterans Stadium (the Vet) in Philadelphia. Playing at the Vet was like coming home for Piazza.

He thrilled his hometown fans, which included friends and family. Piazza crushed a 445-foot home run off pitcher John Smoltz and was named MVP of the 1996 All-Star Game.

In 1997, he hit an amazing .362 and crushed 40 homers. His 201 hits were the most in major-league history by a catcher. Along with Alex Rodriguez, Gary Sheffield, and Mo Vaughn, Piazza was a recipient of the first Ted Williams Greatest Hitters Award sponsored by *Sport Magazine*.

Mike Piazza was named the National League's Rookie of the Year in 1993.

From L.A. to Florida to New York

In the beginning of the 1998 season, the Los Angeles Dodgers made a trade that surprised baseball experts and fans. The Dodgers sent one of their best hitters and most popular players to the Florida Marlins. The player traded was twenty-nine-year-old Mike Piazza. Piazza was known in baseball circles as a "franchise player." That term is used to describe an athlete who can change a team into a winning team that could go on to championships.

The New York Mets wanted a future championship. The Mets quickly arranged to get Piazza from the Florida Marlins.

"When we got Piazza, we gained credibility as a team and as an organization," said Mets general manager Steve Phillips.

Piazza played only 37 games with the Dodgers and 5 with the Florida Marlins in 1998 before being traded. Piazza became a Met on May 23, 1998. How important was that trade? In the year 2000, the Mets published twenty great moments in team history in their stadium yearbook. Listed as one of those moments is the Mike Piazza trade.

In his first 109 games with the Mets, Piazza hit .348, cracked 23 home runs, and drove in 76 runs. One of his homers was the longest home run ever hit at the Houston Astrodome. The ball went about 480 feet. It was hit off pitcher José Lima on September 14, 1998. On September 16, 1998, Piazza smacked the 200th home run of his career, at the Astrodome off pitcher Billy Wagner. When the season ended, Piazza had hit over 30 home runs and collected 100 or more RBIs for the

Mike Piazza was traded by the Dodgers to the Florida Marlins. From the Marlins he went to the New York Mets.

fourth year in a row. He was also well received by his Mets teammates.

"He's the nicest guy in the clubhouse," said former Mets teammate Lenny Harris about Piazza.

The next year Piazza had 162 hits and posted a .303 batting average. He drove in 124 runs for a Mets team record. He belted 40 home runs for the second time in his career. Piazza became the first catcher in major-league history to hit 40 home runs twice during a career.

Most important of all, All-Star catcher Piazza led the New York Mets into the division playoffs in 1999. The Mets earned a wild-card spot by winning a one-game playoff against the Cincinnati Reds. The Mets then played the Arizona Diamondbacks in a best-of-five-game series. The Mets won the series, 3–1, to move on to the NL Championship series. Unfortunately, the Mets lost to the Atlanta Braves, 4–2.

The Mets did not win the National League Championship in 1999 but were not discouraged. They knew that with the help of Piazza a trip to the World Series was just a matter of time. They were right.

The Mets opened the 2000 season by

In May 2000, Mike Piazza hit his 250th home run of his career.

traveling to Tokyo, Japan, to play the Chicago Cubs. It was the first major-league baseball regular season game ever played outside of North America. Unfortunately, the Mets lost, 5–3, to the Cubs that day. The slow-starting Mets went on to lose ten of their first twenty-six games.

Piazza hit third in the batting order for the New York Mets that season. The third slot is usually saved for a team's best hitter. Piazza quickly proved himself to be New York's best hitter. On April 14, 2000, he had a personal best of 5 hits in a single game against the Pittsburgh Pirates. On May 14, he pounded out the 250th home run of his career. It was a grand slam against the Florida Marlins.

In June, Piazza blasted 7 homers, collected 20 batted in, and posted a .375 batting average. One of those 7 homers was a grand slam off pitcher Roger Clemens of the New York Yankees in an inter-league game won by the Mets.

The Subway Series

The 2000 World Series Championship between the N.Y. Mets and the N.Y. Yankees was called a "Subway Series." The Series was called that because fans could ride the subway from Shea Stadium, the home field of the Mets, to Yankee Stadium, the home field of the Yankees.

The 2000 World Series matched up a number of superstar players. The New York Yankees were led by hard-hitting, slick-fielding shortstop Derek Jeter and pitching aces Mariano Rivera and Roger Clemens. The Mets were led by pitching stars Al Leiter and Mike Hampton and superstar catcher Mike Piazza. Based on the past history between Clemens and Piazza, baseball fans eagerly awaited another matchup between the two stars.

Many baseball experts believed Piazza would have the edge when pitcher faced batter. "Piazza is simply the best hitter on either team," wrote one sports reporter.

In the first game of the 2000 Subway Series,

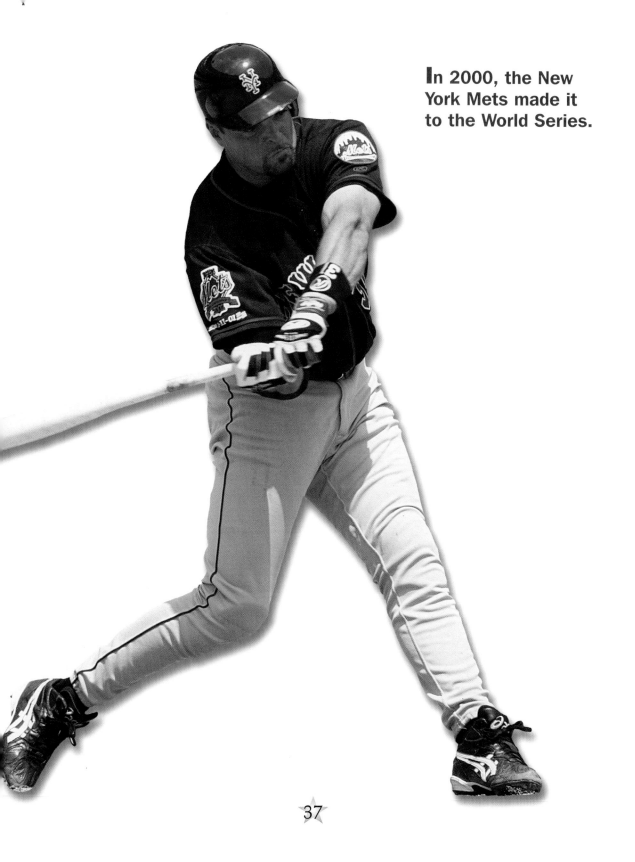

In 2000, the New York Mets made it to the World Series.

the Yankees edged the Mets, 4–3, in twelve innings.

Game Two of the Series was the big matchup between Clemens and Piazza. With Piazza batting for the first time, Clemens fired two fastballs for strikes. The next pitch was a ball. The Yankee ace then threw another strike. Piazza swung hard. He hit a foul ball and shattered his bat. The top of the bat flew toward Clemens. Piazza did not know the ball was foul. He started to run to first. Clemens picked up a piece of the bat and appeared to throw it at the feet of the Mets' star. Piazza started toward Clemens. Clemens moved toward Piazza. Players from both teams rushed onto the field.

Luckily, a fight did not start. Some reporters praised Piazza for not losing his temper. Others questioned his actions.

"I'm in a total no-win situation on that," Piazza explained. "If I fight him and get thrown out, then I'm selfish. And if I do nothing, then I have no guts. It's crazy."

Piazza later hit a homer in the ninth inning of the game off relief pitcher Jeff Nelson. Unfortunately, the Mets lost Game Two to the Yankees, 6–5. Clemens pitched a great game to earn the win. He later explained the bat-throwing incident.

"There was no intent," Clemens said. "I was fired up and emotional and flung the bat toward the on-deck circle where the bat boy was. I had no idea that Mike was running."

The feelings of the Yankee pitchers for Piazza were summed up by then-Yankee pitcher David Cone. "Mike is a classy player," said Cone.

The Mets won Game Three of the Subway Series topping the Yankees, 4–2. Piazza hit a double and scored a run.

The Yankees then won Games Four and Five to win the World Series, 4–1. The Yankees beat the Mets, 3–2, in Game Four, and then, 4–2, in

Game Five. Piazza had 3 hits in 9 at bats in those last two games. In Game Four, he smashed his second home run of the 2000 World Series. Piazza and his teammates lost the 2000 World Series to the powerful N.Y. Yankees. But the Mets were not losers. The Mets were the National League champions. The Mets were winners. So was Mike Piazza.

★★★ UP CLOSE

In 2001, Mike Piazza appeared as a celebrity contestant on the TV quiz show *Jeopardy*. Piazza won the game and donated his cash earnings to teammate Al Leiter's charitable foundation.

"Good Guy"

The N.Y. Mets played the N.Y. Yankees in a three-game inter-league series in June 2002. The Mets won two of those three games. In the second game of the series, Mike Piazza once again stepped up to the plate against Roger Clemens. This time Piazza swung and hit the pitch into the stands for a home run. The Mets won that game, 8–0.

After the game, Piazza was asked about his ongoing duel with Clemens. "I never thought it was personal, but that's just me," Piazza stated. "I've always thought that the game takes care of itself."

Early in the summer of 2003 the N.Y. Yankees took on the N.Y. Mets in inter-league play. Yankee pitcher Roger Clemens had recently notched the 4,000th strikeout and the 300th win of his career against the St. Louis

★★★ UP CLOSE
★

Mike Piazza has always had an interest in music. As a teenager he played electric guitar and drums. Playing the drums is still one of his hobbies. His favorite type of music is heavy metal.

Cardinals on June 13, 2003. Unfortunately, Mike Piazza was not in the Mets' lineup against the Yankees. Piazza had suffered an injury earlier in the year that kept him on the sidelines for the majority of the 2003 season.

Not only is Mike Piazza a great ball player, he likes to help others. Piazza, along with Mets teammates Al Leiter, John Franco, and others, worked as a volunteer carpenter for Habitat for Humanity.

Piazza is also very active in the Mets' "Takin' It to the Fields" program. He makes regular donations to the project that rebuilds ball fields in inner-city areas and helps construct new fields. He is also a member of the American Red Cross National Celebrity Cabinet and was honored in 2001 by the New York Police Athletic League for his actions in the community. In 2002, Piazza received the "Good Guy" award from the New York Chapter of the Baseball Writers' Association. It was a well-deserved honor.

CAREER STATISTICS

	MLB—National League											
Year	Team	G	AB	R	H	2B	3B	HR	RBI	BB	SB	Avg.
1992	LA	21	69	5	16	3	0	1	7	4	0	.232
1993	LA	149	547	81	174	24	2	35	112	46	3	.318
1994	LA	107	405	64	129	18	0	24	92	33	1	.319
1995	LA	112	434	82	150	17	0	32	93	39	1	.346
1996	LA	148	547	87	184	16	0	36	105	81	0	.336
1997	LA	152	556	104	201	32	1	40	124	69	5	.362
1998	LA/FLA/NYM	151	561	88	184	38	1	32	111	58	1	.328
1999	NYM	141	534	100	162	25	0	40	124	51	2	.303
2000	NYM	136	482	90	156	26	0	38	113	58	4	.324
2001	NYM	141	503	81	151	29	0	36	94	67	0	.300
2002	NYM	135	478	69	134	23	2	33	98	57	0	.280
Total		1,393	5,116	851	1,641	251	6	347	1,073	563	17	.321

G—Games
AB—At Bats
R—Runs
H—Hits

2B—Doubles
3B—Triples
HR—Home Runs
RBI—Runs Batted In

BB—Bases on Balls (Walks)
SB—Stolen Bases
Avg.—Batting Average

Where to Write to Mike Piazza

Mr. Mike Piazza
c/o New York Mets
Shea Stadium
123–01 Roosevelt Avenue
Flushing, New York   11368–1699

WORDS TO KNOW

batters' box—Rectangular areas on both sides of the plate. Hitters must stand in those areas to legally hit.

batting average—A player's batting average is determined by dividing the number of at bats the player has into the number of hits a player has.

double—A two-base hit.

grand slam—A home run with runners on first, second, and third base. Four runs are scored on a grand slam.

hit—A ball hit by a batter that is not fielded or is fielded with difficulty and allows the batter to reach base safely.

home run—A fair ball hit out of the playing area and into the stands. It is a four-base hit and is sometimes called a dinger, a round-tripper, or a four-bagger.

manager—The person in charge of handling a professional baseball team and its players. A manager is like a head coach.

minor leagues—Professional baseball leagues that are training grounds for the major leagues. Players learn more about baseball and gain experience playing in the minor leagues.

triple—A three-base hit.

scout—A person who looks at many amateur baseball players to see if they could play professional baseball.

READING ABOUT

Books

Goodman, Michael E. *New York Mets*. Mankato, Minn.: The Creative Company, 2002.

James, Brant and Chelsea House Publishing Staff. *Mike Piazza*. Broomall, Penn.: Chelsea House Publishers, 1997.

Noble, Marty. *Mike Piazza: Mike and the Mets*. Champaign, Ill.: Sports Publishing, 1999.

Owens, Tom. *Mike Piazza: Phenomenal Catcher*. New York: Rosen Publishing Group, 1997.

Samelson, Ken. *Kings of Queens: Amazing Mets Trivia from Stengel to Piazza*. Lenexa, Kan.: Addax Publishing Group, Inc., 2002.

Internet Addresses

ESPN.Com Mike Piazza
<http://baseball.espn.go.com/mlb/players/profile?statsid=4928>

The Official Site of the New York Mets
<http://newyork.mets.mlb.com/NASApp/mlb/index.jsp?c_id=nym>

INDEX